AN EVERY[...]
THE AUTHORI[...] [...]RAPHY OF
MATTHEW IAN TERRY

by Kayla C. Terry

ISBN 1–4196–8191–5

Printed in the U.S.A. by Booksurge.com
Photographs submitted by Teresa Golson, Lindsey Nicholls and Kayla
Terry Family Collection
Graphics and Page Layout by Beth Waltman and Kayla Terry

Books are available at www.amazon.com
and the Rise School of Tuscaloosa

Dedication

I would first like to thank my brother, Ian Terry, for allowing me the pleasure of writing his biography. He truly is my everyday inspiration. I also would like to thank my mother, Teri Terry, for pushing me to be passionate about even the lowliest of tasks. Without them, I would certainly not be who I am today and I dedicate this biography to both of them.

Ian and his mother, Teri

Acknowledgements

Gene Stallings

Gary Shores

Lane and Faye Hubbard

Bart Cannon

Jessica Robertson

Kaye Guthrie

Teresa Golson

Dr. Martha Cook

Dr. Carol Bishop Mills

Meredith Cummings

The Rise School

Crossing Points

Juanita Dyer

Beth Waltman

Lindsey Nicholls

Contents

A Foreword by Coach Gene Stallings

While reading Kayla Terry's book about growing up with Ian, I was reminded of Johnny and his four sisters. The girls perceived Johnny as their brother and not so much as someone with Down syndrome. As with Kayla, he was especially close to his sisters; they were buddies and to this day maintain that unique relationship. All the girls were very protective of Johnny. Ruth Ann and I never had to worry about someone being cruel or mean to Johnny because the girls would protect him. They included him in their lives to the extent that having Down syndrome wasn't Johnny's sole identity. Their acceptance of their brother filtered down to their friends and our extended family. As the girls became older and started dating, accepting Johnny was the litmus test for dates. If you were uncomfortable around him, you didn't come back. In many ways Johnny has shaped all their lives and transcended generations. He has many nieces and nephews whom he dearly loves, and they dearly love him. I admire Kayla for being able to write this book and I hope that it makes its way into many school libraries. Tolerance and acceptance are hard lessons to teach and maybe this book will help reach those who need a true account of these values.

Gene Stallings

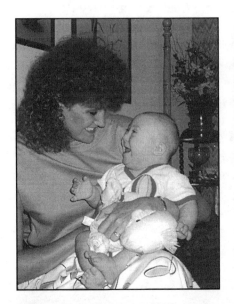

From top left:
Ian and Mom share a laugh
Ian and Kayla
Dad, Kayla and Ian
Stuart, Ian and Mom

Chapter One
"My Name is Matthew Ian Terry."

Matthew Ian Terry, born October 26, 1986, in Tuscaloosa, Alabama, is a young man who has accomplished many things that were thought to be impossible. He was born with Down syndrome, a genetic disorder caused by the presence of an extra twenty-first chromosome that causes impairment of cognitive ability and physical growth as well as facial appearance. Ian's parents, Johnny and Teri Terry, always believed in Ian's success and pushed him farther than anyone ever expected him to go. Ian has two younger siblings: a sister, named Kayla, and a brother, named Stuart. He still resides in his hometown of Northport, Alabama, and continues to break preconceived notions of the special needs community.

Ian's senior portrait

Chapter Two
Special Delivery

On October 26, 1986, after months of anticipation, Johnny and Teri Terry had their first child, Matthew Ian Terry. They had been married for a little over a year and were thrilled to begin their family together. "We wanted to have the first boy in our family. We were so excited. It was a perfect pregnancy," Teri recalled. "I was a young mother. I was in good health and there was no indication that my baby would be anything but perfect."

The day after Ian was born, the pediatrician entered the room and asked for Mrs. Thompson. When Teri told the doctor she was not Mrs. Thompson, but Mrs. Terry, and asked if he had examined her son, the doctor replied, "Yes, he's retarded." Confused and hurt, Teri

Ian and his parents, Johnny and Teri

could not believe that this was true. She asked if Ian was going to die, and the doctor said, "No, he has Down syndrome." Teri had heard of this condition before but didn't know exactly what it meant. The situation was made worse because her husband was not there. Johnny had left to go to the store to buy celebratory cigars, so she had to break the news to him. She recalled, "I didn't even know if it was true or not. I was just in denial."

The social worker from the hospital met with the new parents to discuss their options for their son. They were told that Ian could be put up for adoption or be placed in an institution. To this Johnny replied, "We came here to have a baby and we're leaving here with a baby. He's our baby." Teri was then segregated from other mothers at the hospital for fear that she would "upset" them. She was not allowed to attend the new mothers' class but instead was given private instruction. To add insult to injury, she was given an outdated "informational brochure" on Mongoloids.

The Terrys' ordeal at the hospital was finally over when they were released two days after Ian was born. Johnny and Teri took Ian to Birmingham, Alabama, to confirm Ian's diagnosis with a genetic specialist. The specialist said that there was no possible way that it could have been prevented. "They basically told us to take him home and love him, and that's what we did." After a week of caring for Ian, Johnny and Teri realized that the only thing that was different about what they expected parenting would be like was themselves. "I thought that everything was going to be so different since I had Ian, but I realized that I was doing the same things I would have been doing," Teri said,

"Whenever something like that happens, the first thing you need to do is lick your own wounds. You have to deal with it yourself before you can open up to other people."

Many instances in Ian's life seem to occur miraculously in his favor. The first of these events, and the first glimmer of hope for the Terrys, happened shortly after Ian's birth. His father, Johnny, was going to inform his sister, Jackie, about Ian's condition and ask her to accompany him to break the news to his mother. Jackie works at the University of Alabama in the Rose Administration Building. Betsy Gary, who also works at the University, decided to walk to the Rose Administration Building instead of her usual routine of having

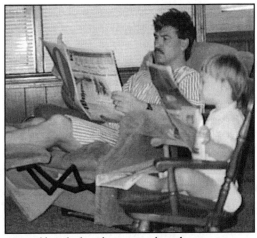

Ian and his dad, Johnny, reading the paper

a student retrieve her mail the very same day Johnny was going to Rose. Betsy Gary had been a high school classmate of Johnny's and also had a Down syndrome son two years earlier. Coincidentally, Johnny found Jackie, and Betsy in conversation, neither knowing why Johnny was there. He asked, "Are you Betsy Gary?" When she confirmed, he said, "I just had a son yesterday born with Down syndrome. Do you have time to talk to me?" Betsy was very kind and informative, and she assured Johnny that the perfect place for Ian would be the RISE Program, or Rural Infant Stimulation Environment. It was after his conversation with Betsy that Johnny was inspired and relieved. Help was on the way. He was able to return to the hospital with confidence, and he reassured his wife that they were going to be fine.

The youngest child to have ever been enrolled at Rise, Ian began his education at eleven days old. Rise is a program designed for young children, from birth to five years, with special needs. Rise develops an individualized plan to help enhance the development of its students to reach their goals in a timelier manner. They also concentrate on the entire family. Rise not only helps the student, but they help parents understand and cope with their child's disability. They provide information and instruction to the parents that enables them to better help their child.

Rise was the initial location of Ian exceeding expectations. Ian quickly emerged as a leader among his peers. He showed a love of learning that surprised everyone. "He never gave up. He always gave a hundred and ten percent in whatever he did," his mother remembers. Because of his accomplishments, Ian was always a teacher's favorite. These special instructors knew that Ian was exceptional and was rewriting the standards for a child with Down syndrome. Even at an early age, Ian

Ian's Rise graduation portrait

7

was recognized by many in the special education field. He received the "Yes, I Can" award in 1990 for his academic successes. In 1994, the Rise School constructed a new building and dedicated one of the classrooms in Ian's name.

By the time Ian graduated from the Rise School when he was five years old, he had learned to cut, color, snip, paste, and recite his numbers and ABCs. He was more than prepared for kindergarten. "Even though I was very excited about Ian's pending graduation from the Rise School, I was apprehensive about the next phase he was about to enter," his mother remembers. "Rise had become a safe haven, an environment where he was totally accepted and we were totally accepted. We had grown to depend on their support, but we had to have faith and confidence in what we all had learned. It was time for us to move on."

Ian with Rise Director, Dr. Martha Cook

Chapter Three
"I'm the Big Brother."

When Ian was a little over a year old, his parents were trying to decide whether it was time for Ian to have a brother or sister. After Johnny and Teri revisited the genetics specialist in Birmingham, Alabama, and determined that it wasn't likely that Down syndrome would be an issue again, they decided that having another baby would be the best thing for themselves and Ian.

In October 1988, Ian not only celebrated his second birthday, but he celebrated the birth of his new baby sister, Kayla. Three days after Ian blew out his candles, he went to see his sister for the very first time. "I was happy." Ian said. "I wanted to be a big brother." The new addition to the family seemed to improve Ian's maturity. His sister became a motivation for Ian to grow up and be "a big boy." Having a sister was beneficial for his development. Ian and Kayla became tagalong companions and followed each other everywhere. Alone, Ian may have been hesitant to explore or try new things, but with his sister at his side, he could do anything. "Me and my sister still spend quality time together. Kayla is my sister and my friend."

In October of 1992, the Terrys had another addition to the family: Ian's younger brother, Stuart. Since Ian was so close in age to his sister, he didn't have the typical "Big Brother" role until Stuart was born. "I always told Stuart what to do. I'm his big brother so he has to get my permission. I always tell him to clean his room, do his homework, do his chores, but he's my buddy, too."

With the birth of all three of the Terry children in the month of October, it became a particularly special month. Ian's mom, Teri, said, "It was everyone's birthday and Halloween all together so the whole month of October seemed to be full of celebration, costumes, and parties. The three of them usually had one birthday party at home with our extended family,

and one at the venue of their choice, so I would plan at least six parties that month, not including Halloween."

The "Bat-Terrys" prepare to fight crime

Halloween has proven to be a Terry family specialty and a favorite holiday for Ian. "I love to trick or treat, but my costume is always my favorite part of Halloween." Throughout the years Ian has been a Ninja Turtle, Buzz Lightyear, The Red Power Ranger, Spiderman, a Skeleton, and Elvis. One special year, Ian decided he wanted to be Batman. He said, "Batman is a leader, and a leader needs sidekicks. Let's fight some crime." Ian coerced Kayla and Stuart to be Batgirl and Robin. The "Bat–Terrys" wore their costumes to the Rise School's Halloween party and posed with the children.

Chapter Four
Breaking Barriers

After an emotional roller coaster during the first six years of Ian Terry's life, it was time for him to move forward in his education. The Rise Program had seen him through birth and prepared him for elementary school. Ian's parents were confident in his success in a public school, but others were not so certain. "I thought that people of authority were experts, but I quickly learned that was not the case. My expectations of school administrators was that they would do what was best by Ian and do what was right for him," Ian's mother later recalled. "I was disappointed many times."

When they met with the school's principal for the first time, he was anything but supportive to the idea of having a Down syndrome child begin kindergarten at his school. Teri and Johnny took Ian's case to the Tuscaloosa County School Board and were successful in obtaining permission, even though it was already a known law that students should be placed in their least restrictive environments. Prior to Ian, no one had challenged the system to change, and he was the first child with Down syndrome to be educated in a regular class setting in the public school system.

Once this barrier had been lifted, Ian became an encouragement to others in the special needs community. Many parents and students followed suit and it became clear to teachers that having Ian in their classrooms was a great advantage. In the months leading up to school, many teachers would contact Ian and his parents requesting to have Ian in their room for the year. Ian had many great and supportive teachers and PARA professionals over the years. "I knew it was different and challenging for Ian to be in a regular classroom setting, but so many teachers rose to the challenge and we were always grateful for their efforts," Ian's mother said.

During his seven years in grade school, Ian's learning abilities exceeded everyone's expectations. By the sixth grade, he could read, do mathematics, write and sign his whole name in cursive, and he was a constant fixture on the A Honor Roll. Not only did Ian learn a lot during this time, but he taught others as well. Many of Ian's classmates had never encountered someone with special needs, let alone Down syndrome. Ian proved to be a social butterfly and gained friendships very easily. On one or two occasions, however, some classmates were not so considerate. One afternoon Ian returned home with red ink marks all over the back of his shirt; they had come from a bully at his school who had written on him. Although he was discouraged at times by such behavior, he continued to move forward and didn't let it affect his education or friendships with others.

Ian played sports and participated in other activities as any young individual does. Ian found it hard to stick to an activity when he was younger. Throughout his young life, Ian has been in karate, the Boy Scouts, gymnastics, and the ROTC. He and his sister played on the YMCA tee–ball team that their dad coached. However, he did not participate for very long in this activity, because it did not interest him. At his tee–ball games, Ian would usually hit one ball and then decide he was too tired to play the rest of the game and wanted to enjoy his team drink. He would sit in the stands and cheer on his teammates. Much to their father's disappointment, Ian and Kayla were the two least interested players on the team. Ian's interest in an activity may have fluctuated, but no matter how many times he became bored with an activity, his parents continually allowed him to try something new just like his peers.

One interest that has withstood the test of time is Ian's love of music and celebrities; he is constantly researching his favorite musicians and always keeps tabs on what they are up to. One singer in particular has been Ian's favorite since her debut: country music singer

Ian meets with LeAnn Rimes

LeAnn Rimes. Ian has collected every album, poster, t–shirt, and book about the singer and is an avid member of her fan club. Because of his membership, Ian has won an outfit worn by LeAnn on her tour and has met her on several occasions. He has been such a constant figure at her private fan club parties that she now recognizes him and calls him by name. LeAnn's mother has even called him "Sweetie Pie," and he has had the opportunity to meet and talk with LeAnn's husband, Dean, on many occasions.

Another celebrity obsession of Ian's has been the King himself, Elvis Presley. Ian likes to capture parts of Elvis' persona into his own, for example: being a ladies' man, singing songs, having droves of screaming fans, and dancing like there's no tomorrow. Ian was un-aware, however, of one particular occurrence in Elvis' life: his death. Ian had bought the Elvis made–for–TV movie about the life and times of the King of Rock 'n' Roll to watch with his best friend, Ben Sanford. Ian's mother was downstairs when she heard banging and cries coming from Ian's room. "I ran upstairs because I thought they were hurt. When I went in Ian's room, Ben and Ian were hugging and crying." Teri asked what had happened and Ian cried, "He's dead, Momma! Elvis is dead!"

Ian and his best friend, Ben Sanford

Chapter Five
Little Brother

When Ian's younger brother, Stuart, was in the fourth grade, their mother received a phone call from one of Stuart's teachers. This was something that worried Teri since a phone call from one of Stuart's teachers was usually not a good thing. This particular call was one of praise, however.

Stuart's teacher, Mrs. Frannie, began to explain to Teri about what had happened that day. Teri wondered what he had done this time; Stuart's classroom behavior record was sometimes not very enviable. Mrs. Frannie told Teri about her lesson for that day. The class had been studying the Dark Ages, Kings, Queens, and Court Jesters. She explained to her students that sometimes during the Dark Ages, Kings would keep jesters around to laugh at and use as entertainment. In those days, dwarves and mentally handicapped people would find employment by allowing people to laugh at them and thus become court jesters. At that very moment Stuart stood up and firmly said "That is so wrong!" The class became quiet and all eyes stared intently at Stuart. He paused, looked around the room, and continued, "I have a brother who is special, and he is so wonderful. It would break my heart if anyone used him to laugh at." Mrs. Frannie said he was such a proud brother; she was rendered speechless. She could hardly find the words to follow such a sincere confession of love. He educated every single student in the room. The lesson that Stuart taught his fellow students was far greater than the one she had actually planned.

Ian with his younger brother, Stuart

Chapter Six
"Pizza Power!"

Ian Terry's favorite food is indisputably pizza. He eats it at least ten times a week, for lunch or dinner or both. Pizza has been a major part of Ian's life since a very young age. When asked about his favorite meal he says, "It makes me feel good; it's good for my health. I like sausage and pepperoni the best because they taste the best." The taste only explains a small reason why eating pizza has become a daily habit for Ian. It all began in Pre–School when Ian and his younger sister, Kayla, would get ready each morning. They would both wake up and get dressed in their parents' room, usually while watching television. One day, a television program appeared that would forever change Ian's eating habits: Teenage Mutant Ninja Turtles. The crime–fighting turtle ninjas kept the streets of Manhattan safe and would often celebrate over a slice of pizza. The show quickly became Ian's favorite and forever changed his diet. "Turtles have pizza power; I wanted pizza power!" he explained. Although Ian has learned to appreciate and try different foods – like chicken, hamburgers, and even escargot – he still chooses pizza as his favorite delicacy.

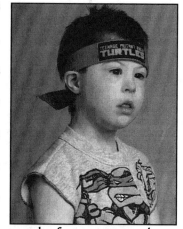

Ian in his favorite Ninja Turtle outfit

Chapter Seven
Honesty is the Best Policy

If there is one thing Ian is good at, it's being completely honest, even if it creates an awkward situation. One of these now infamous occurrences was at a family reunion. The food had been eaten and all the small talk had been said, and it was time to say goodbye to everyone. Ian's mother, Teri, was exchanging words with one particular distant

relative that had hosted the reunion when Ian decided to tell her good-bye. "He came up and gave her a hug," Teri remembers, "and I told him to say 'Thank you for the food and I had a good time.' The relative in return said, "You are welcome anytime, Ian." Then Ian said, "Thank you, sir."" Ian's mother corrected him, "No, Ian, Thank you ma'am." It was then that Ian disagreed and said, "No, Mom, Thank you sir. They have a mustache!" Although embarrassment has not kept the Terry family from their family re-

Ian is packed and ready for anything

unions, they still try to avoid Aunt Mustachio.

Another situation where Ian caused some embarrassment to his mother was at a school meeting with one of Ian's new teachers. The woman had a very elaborate hairstyle that Ian had never encountered before. Teri knew that this hair would evoke some response out of Ian. As she nervously sat through the meeting, Ian didn't say anything about the woman's hair, although she could tell he was in deep thought about it. "I admittedly was intrigued by the hairstyle," Teri said. "It looked plastic and stood up at least two feet; kind of like Marge Simpson. I knew it would be hard for Ian to resist a comment." Surprisingly, the meeting finished without any mortification. However, when Ian's mother thought she had gotten away with no comments about the hair, Ian looked admiringly at the woman and asked, "Can I try on your wig?"

Stuart, Ian and Kayla

Needless to say, Ian can cause a few awkward moments that end with a laugh, but many of Ian's honest moments can be deep and inspiring. After a long, stressful and rainy day at the office, Ian's mother picked him up from school. "All I could think about was how terrible my day had been," Teri recalled. She felt that it should be against the law for people to get out in such bad weather. One single thought that came from her son completely changed her day. Ian got in the car, "I love the rain!" Ian said with a smile. His mother retorted, "And why do you love the rain so much?" He simply replied, "God made the rain. I love the rain. Don't you love the rain, Mom?" And, of course, his mom agreed. These moments make him special. One could never imagine that someone with such a simple grasp of the world's concepts could be so right. With a single word or smile, Ian has the ability to change a person's outlook and mood to a feeling of happiness. People simply enjoy being around him. His smile and laugh are simply magical.

Ian in crib after a nap

Chapter Eight
A Friend in God

Insensitivity can definitely rear its ugly head when it is least expected. There is a moral obligation felt by families and friends of those with special needs to protect and stand up to this insensitivity. Ian's mother, Teri, explains that "people as a whole don't intentionally hurt others' feelings, especially people like Ian. They just need to be enlightened and educated."

Going to Sunday morning church has become a favorite activity for Ian, especially contemporary worship services, or as he calls it, "Karaoke Church," since the music is modern and the lyrics are projected on a big screen. On one particular Sunday, the message was about diligence in prayer and making time for God. The minister urged the congregation to set aside a time for a quiet, peaceful talk with the Lord everyday and not to be a "RETARD" in your prayer. This particular word had been used numerous times by a few of Ian's tormentors and bullies from school and on the bus, so it was extremely shocking to Teri to hear that word come out of the minister's mouth. "I looked over at Ian, and the hurt and confusion on his face cut through my heart like a knife," Teri said, "I could see his facial expression and posture change; he was hurt and sad." Ian and his mother decided to leave the service, and walked hand in hand down the aisle of the church.

Later that day, the Terry family received many calls of support and love from their congregation, but more importantly, a call of apology was received. Teri and the minister had a long talk. "I think we reached an understanding of how hurtful his words were. He assured me that he would never again say that and he too would teach others about how hurtful this word can be." The following Sunday, Ian and his mother sat and talked with the humbled minister, when he asked for Ian's forgiveness. Ian simply asked, "Do you want to be a bully on the bus, or a friend in God?" When the minister replied, "A friend in God," Ian said, "Then I forgive you because that is what Jesus says to do."

Grannie Dyer and Ian ready for
LeAnn Rimes concert.

Chapter Nine

"I'm a Teenager."

In the fall of 2002, Ian Terry became a freshman at Tuscaloosa County High School. He was finally a self–proclaimed "teenager" and was very proud of that fact. He reminded everyone in his family daily of his teenage angst, although it was never that serious. He went through what every average teenage person goes through, like school dances, having a crush, and going to football games. Ian even got his learner's permit to drive. "I wanted to learn; I had to drive like my sister does. I was a little bit nervous because my sister, Kayla, is a good driver and I wasn't a very careful driver. I studied my drivers' book for a long

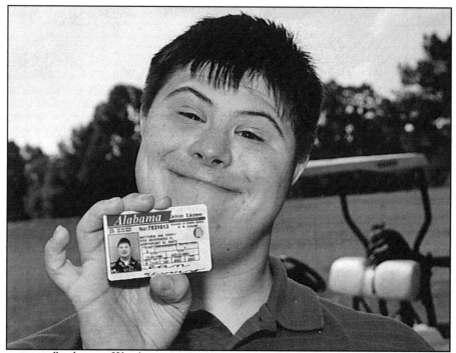

Ian proudly shows off his learner's permit

time. I took the test and got it! I didn't make an A, but I made a B. Now I have an ID like the FBI."

Ian has been allowed behind the wheel only a few times. The one person who was brave enough to sit in the passenger seat was Ian's grandfather, Lane Hubbard, also known as Papa. "He knows how to use the gas very well," Hubbard has said. "He needs to work on the brakes a little bit more." After his driving lessons, Ian felt confident enough to drive a go-cart at an amusement park during a family vacation to Gulf Shores, Alabama. Ian and his siblings each hopped into a go–cart and began their laps. After the standard four or five laps, a park staffer waved the flag to alert the drivers of their last lap. All the drivers slowed their go-carts into the pit – all except Ian. Ian decided that his turn was not over. He kept speeding around the track while the park

Ian receiving an award for his contribution to the All-American City Awards with the mayors of Tuscaloosa and Northport

staff tried to stop Ian's go-cart. "I didn't know how to go slow, only fast," Ian said. After Ian made fools out of every park staffer that attempted to catch him, he accidentally crashed his go-cart into a pile of broken-down carts. "[The owners] were very mad and rude about the go-carts. We can't go back now." Since this incident, Ian has not driven a motorized vehicle.

Ian continued to become more and more popular not only at school, but also in his surrounding community. Ian and his family were chosen to travel to Kansas City, Missouri, to represent Rise School graduates and their families at the All–American City Awards. He prepared a short speech for the presentation and spoke in front of hundreds of people at the competition. Many felt that Tuscaloosa gained the pres-

Ian and his castmates from *The Wizard of Oz*

tigious title of being an All–American City because of Ian and how well he represented the Rise School. This event sparked a new passion for Ian that he still carries on today: performing for an audience.

Since he was a boy, Ian has always enjoyed singing and dancing to his favorite songs. As a matter of fact, Ian improved his reading skills by playing with his Karaoke machine almost every day. It wasn't until his high school days that he showed interest in doing theatre. He had attended a summer drama program called Mel–O–Drama with his sister, brother, and cousins. He worked hard and learned a lot about theatre etiquette, but never had a big part in the final production. "I was a little bit jealous of my sister, brother, and cousins" he said, "They were in plays and I wasn't. I wanted to be a star, too." Once he heard that Tuscaloosa Children's Theatre would be performing *The Wizard of Oz*, he knew that this would be his big break. He prepared his audition material for months, and when the day came, he knew he was ready. He performed an Elvis classic for the audition: "You Ain't Nothin' but a Hound Dog." After his audition, he anxiously awaited the cast list to be posted. Ian recalled being "a little bit nervous. I wanted to be in *The Wizard of Oz* very much." When the cast list was posted and Ian's name appeared on it as an Ozian and Winkie Guard, he was overwhelmed with joy. "I was very happy and excited," he said, "Now I can be a star."

Over the months of rehearsal, the entire cast got to know Ian and was very impressed with his acting abilities. News about Ian went around town and soon he was interviewed by the *Tuscaloosa News*. To everyone's surprise, the article appeared on the front page of the newspaper. Ian knew he now had become a star, at least in Tuscaloosa.

Ian's performance as an Ozian impressed his family and friends. He had caught the acting bug. Ian decided to focus on his next ambition: *High School Musical*. The Disney Channel movie about two teens who share a love for music had become Ian's new obsession. "I wanted to be in the movie; I wanted to be Troy Bolton, the lead," Ian said. Ian engulfed his life in all things related to *High School Musical*. He learned every song and dance step, collected books and soundtracks from the movie, and dreamed about one day being in *High School Musical*. Coincidentally, Tuscaloosa County High School was planning to perform

Ian and his castmates from *High School Musical*

High School Musical as their spring production. Ian's dream would come true. His reputation from the *Wizard of Oz* had followed him as he once again impressed the director with his skills. While he was just an Ozian in his last performance, he was now a named character with two lines. Although he didn't get the part of Troy Bolton, Ian was still happy that his dream of being in his favorite play came true. Ian's younger brother, Stuart, said it best that "although he wasn't chosen to be the star of the play, at times, he was."

Ian graduated from high school in the spring of 2005. He had finally completed the three major stages of education: elementary, middle, and high school, but the question arose as to what he was to do next. "I wanted to go to college to the University of Alabama," Ian said. Thanks to the CrossingPoints program at the University of Alabama, he was able to attend the Capstone.

Ian with his date to the Prom, Heather

Chapter Ten
Family

Family has always been an important aspect of Ian's life. Since the time Ian and his two younger siblings, Kayla and Stuart, were very young, their parents stressed the importance of loving your family unconditionally. Not only has Ian been lucky enough to have supportive parents and siblings, but he also has a strong extended family that loves him. Ian has an especially close relationship with his mother's parents, Lane and Faye Hubbard. "If there had been a cure for Down syndrome when Ian was born, my mother would have found it," Ian's mother, Teri, said. "She tried so hard to learn everything she could about it. In the end, it didn't matter because she still loves him just the way he is."

The Hubbards, lovingly referred to as Papa and Nana, have always provided Ian with a second home. Ian usually spends at least half of the week at his grandparents' house. When asked why he enjoys his Nana and Papa's house so much, Ian simply replies that he "loves Nana

Ian and Nana

and Papa," but his sister Kayla seems to think it's another reason. "He gets to be the only child. He loves to be spoiled. When he stays with us, he's just another kid in the house, but at Nana and Papa's, he's the one and only." Besides spoiling him, Lane and Faye have taught Ian how to shave, how to drive, and how to dress like a man, mostly an older man because of his grandfather's influence upon his wardrobe.

Ian represents the center of his family. His mother, father, siblings, grandparents, aunts, uncles, and cousins all support and love Ian. He brings out the best of the whole family; he unites and strengthens them. The family has found that they needed him in their lives more than he needed them. He is considered a blessing.

There is a significant difference in the life Ian's family had envisioned and the life they are actually living. Teri has said, "I know in my heart that our life rewards are greater than any of us ever dreamed they would be. We as a family have been blessed."

Ian and his family at Nana and Papa's 50th Wedding Anniversary

Chapter Eleven
"Let us Pray."

If there's one thing that Ian's family has learned to have, it is Faith, and no one has as good a grasp upon it as Ian. He always leads the family in prayer, and always insists upon everyone holding hands while saying grace. In the early days of Ian's prayer, it usually had nothing to do with giving thanks to God or blessing the food he was about to eat. Instead, he prayed for his favorite country music stars, like Billy Gillman and LeAnn Rimes, his best friend, Ben Sanford, or whatever girl he had a crush on that week. Eventually, Ian's spiritual maturity grew and so did his desire to be baptized.

On one particular Sunday at church, a new member was getting baptized. Ian had never seen this ceremony before, and it sparked a new obsession with baptism in Ian. Ian had many questions, but Teri wanted to make sure he fully understood the commitment and what it means to be baptized. The next week at church, Ian kept bothering his mother during the service. "When is my turn? I need to be baptized. Is it today? I need to be baptized!" he said. When his mother explained that he had to have a meeting with the pastor before he could be baptized, Ian decided to take matters into his own hands. "Fine, I'll do it myself!" He walked out of the service to the bathroom and did not return until a few moments later. When he sat down at his seat, his mother realized that he had soaked his entire head in the bathroom and was now completely drenched with water from the neck up. He had baptized himself. A few weeks later, Ian met with his favorite pastor, Michael, and had his "real" baptism ceremony the next Sunday.

Once again, Ian shows that no matter how simple a person may seem, what lies within can be deep and profound. His beliefs and faith in God are inspirational. In today's world, religion has become so evolved and so branched away from its true meaning, but Ian can remind us what it really is all about, "I love God. I love Jesus. They love me."

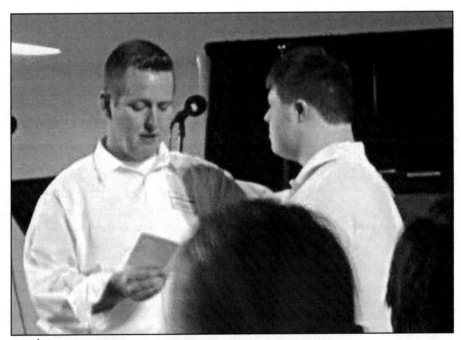

Ian's baptism ceremony

Chapter Twelve

"I'm a Man."

Ian was now an adult. While many special needs parents decide that going from kindergarten through twelfth grade is enough, Ian's parents knew that graduation was not the end of Ian's education. Ian was still learning and growing intellectually. He began attending CrossingPoints two years prior to his graduation and once again, was the youngest student, having been enrolled at seventeen. He was still officially a county student, but attended classes at the University. CrossingPoints is a collaboration between the University of Alabama's College of Education and the Tuscaloosa City and County School Systems.

Ian and former UA coach, Gene Stallings

It provides transition services for students ages eighteen to twenty–one years old with disabilities. Students participating in CrossingPoints receive hands–on instruction in basic day–to–day living and employment skills. Students are placed in specially selected or designed job sites at the University of Alabama.

Ian's first job at the Paul "Bear" Bryant Museum not only helped him gain knowledge about the Alabama Crimson Tide, but also sparked a new life–long friendship with his supervisor, Gary Shores. Ian worked in the archives department in the museum with Shores, restoring old footage of Crimson Tide athletics dating as far back as the 1920s. Everyone quickly learned that Ian's work ethic was incomparable. When asked about Ian's efforts, Shores said, "Ian is extremely smart and extremely competitive. When he is given a challenge, that's when he shines." Ian soon mastered the skills of transferring old footage to DVD, editing digital footage, and creating web pages, and he has even

interviewed Jack Rutledge, former University of Alabama assistant football coach, and Gene Stallings, one of Alabama's most beloved football coaches, to practice his interview and speaking skills. Ian has hopes of interviewing many other community leaders, sports figures,

Ian worked with archives and old film at his job at the Paul "Bear" Bryant Museum and other people he finds interesting. "He learned everything on his own; I just gave him the basics and he has just taken it into his own hands," said Shores. "He has challenged me to be a harder worker. It's been fun working with Ian. That's what's missing in the workplace today - fun."

Ian is a very loyal person and reserves his summer employment to return to his beloved alma mater, The Rise School. He is employed as a classroom teacher assistant. Ian helps with the daily classroom activities, assists with meal preparation and occasionally reads to the classroom. He also likes to deliver the mail and shred documents for his boss and family friend Dr. Martha Cook, Director of Rise. The children see him as an authority figure and refer to him affectionately as Mr. Ian. Ian's presence is also an inspiration to new parents of special needs infants. Ian is hope for the next generation.

Gary Shores and Ian

Conclusion
"Thank you. Thank you very much."

Ian's life so far has just been the beginning. He still has many dreams and ambitions for which he strives. The possibilities of Ian's future are endless. When asked about Ian's possible careers, Gary Shores thinks Ian could be a television station camera man or a behind–the–scenes editor. Whatever path Ian chooses to take, it is certain that he will be one thing: a role model. "Ian is an example of what can be done," says Shores. It's anyone's guess what Ian will be doing in the next five, ten, or even twenty years, but Ian is sure of his own future. "I want to be famous… I want to be a peacemaker and help people. One day, I hope there is an Ian Terry Museum."

Ian has always lived by the words of former University of Alabama coach Paul "Bear" Bryant, "Surround yourself with good people." The people that have surrounded Ian in his lifetime all have had some sort of influence on him, just as he has had an influence on them. He continues to inspire and give hope to those who encounter him, including me. Through life's many experiences and challenges, he has taught me to be compassionate, to believe in myself, and above all, he has taught me to laugh and love life. For someone who appears to have limited potential, he actually has unlimited possibilities. Because of

Ian's attitude, when I am met with a challenge that seems impossible, I think of all of his accomplishments and his determination to succeed. I doubt that anyone that has met Ian would have been the same person without him. His smile alone is enough to change someone's mood. Ian is and will always be an everyday inspiration to me and to those who surround him and are fortunate enough to experience Matthew Ian Terry.

"Thank you. Thank you very much!"

About the Rise School

On October 1, 1974, Rise was funded by the U.S. Office of Health, Education and Welfare as a demonstration program designed to serve young children with physical disabilities from birth to five years of age. Located in one room of a house on the campus of The University of Alabama, Rise served six young children with a staff that consisted of a teacher, a teacher assistant and a family service coordinator. After three years of federal funding, The University of Alabama funded the program in 1977. The focus of the program expanded to include more diversity in enrollment, and in addition, to children with cerebral palsy and spina bifida, Rise served children with Down syndrome and other developmental disabilities.

By 1986, the program had expanded to include 60 children with dis-

abilities and their typically developing peers. The funding of the program became a combination of support from the University, state contracts and grants, interagency agreements, fundraisers and private donors.

In 1990, Gene Stallings became the head football coach at The University of Alabama and immediately became an advocate for the Rise School. His son, Johnny, was born with Down syndrome in 1962 when Stallings was an assistant football coach at Alabama for the legendary Paul "Bear" Bryant. Having little or no support when Johnny was born, Coach Stallings and his wife, Ruth Ann appreciated the availability of the services provided by the Rise School. In 1991, a special employment program was initiated that provided jobs to adults with Down syndrome. In 1992, The University of Alabama began a capital campaign that included

a new facility for the Rise School. The Rise School met its goal and the new facility, The Stallings Center opened on November 30, 1994. Since that time, the program has expanded to include six classrooms serving 80 children.

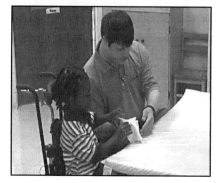

Opposite and right:
Ian working with Rise students

About CrossingPoints

CrossingPoints is a collaboration between The University of Alabama's Interdisciplinary Teacher Education Department in the College of Education and the Tuscaloosa City and County Schools Systems. The purpose of CrossingPoints is to provide transition services for students with disabilities ages eighteen to twenty-one. Students participating in CrossingPoints receive hands–on instruction in vocational/employment aspects of transition during their job placement in specially selected or designed jobs sites at The University of Alabama. The students spend up to four hours a day, four days a week in real–job setting while receiv-

CrossingPoints students Bradley and Patty

Ian and his CrossingPoints classmates before their Prom

ing instruction in employ-ment–related skills. The CrossingPoints transition model helps employers better understand the realities and advantages of hiring people with disabilities. Classroom

Ian with his classmate Nate

instruction is also provided in the area of functional academics.

"We gotta go, we got things to do."

Made in the USA